Sylvia Plath came to prominence, in both life and death, during a time when poets were still a literary elite, when some of them could turn into minor media stars and, in the spirit of Percy Bysshe Shelley and William Blake, act as provocateurs of cultural revolution. Ones with enough confidence could thrill large audiences, confront the establishment and develop decadent lustres almost like their jazz bop collaborators and, later, sycophantic rock and roll friends.

Plath never did any of that but, while many poets of that generation have faded from public awareness, her rare poetic genius and tragic early death brought an iconic and controversial fame.

***

The wind pours by

like destiny

Sylvia Plath,

Asa Benveniste,

and the poetic afterlife

Jay Jeff Jones

Enquiries to **Alternative Culture Studies**

Altcult101@gmail.com

Printed in the United States of America
First Printing: 2022

Unbalanced Books
ISBN- 9798837457531

It's a late winter's afternoon on the top of Cross Hill, with Hardcastle Crags[i] on one side and Colden Valley on the other. Down in their depths of hibernating trees and gritstone slabs, darkness isn't coming down – it's rising like a cold damp tide. The uplands are a stonewalled pattern of vacant fields and meadows and the faraway moors look grey and barren. From the red tension on the horizon comes not warmth but a wind hardened on the edges of Atlantic storm waves. This is the natural landscape for tough history, for subsistence hill farming, cradle-to-grave mill working, adversity waiting around every corner and a whole lot of outlawry.

From here, it's a short walk to Heptonstall,[ii] a village of medieval origin with two churches, one chapel and three graveyards. In the oldest of these, the bone strata measure out centuries, with periods crowded into short lives, taken by plague and consumption. At times, the dead bell could have been tied to a metronome. Childhood here was a time of special peril - as noted by Ken Smith in his poem "Colden Valley" – 'And all its children gone through millyards / into stone they chiselled *Billy, Emma, Jack,* / and gave their dates and shut the ground'. The poet Sylvia Plath once refused to live nearby and, if she had been asked, was unlikely to have chosen this village as her final resting place.

Early in Plath's marriage to Ted Hughes, when they were financially struggling emergent poets, he suggested that they should buy an old manor house somewhere in the socially depressed Calder Valley. They were seated at the bar of the Stubbing Wharf, what was then a shabby public house on the edge of the town of Hebden Bridge. He had renamed the same place 'Top Wharf' in his short story "Sunday", recalling an après-chapel, boyhood experience where the sport was terrier dogs killing captive rats in the pub yard. A local 'simpleton', Billy Red, would bite off rats' heads in return for pints of ale. For child Ted, who had been born not far down the road, this stark memory was part of being conditioned to rustic, manly amusements where the object is death.

In "Stubbing Wharfe", the poem he wrote about the much later conversation with Plath, Hughes gave the pub interior a fatal mood of 'shut-in sodden dreariness'. One of the properties he had in mind was Lumb Bank, a rambling, former mill owner's house located in the Colden Valley. It was only half an hour's walk from where they were sitting. Conveniently, to his thinking, the narrow, steep lane that passed Lumb Bank's front gate came out next to The Beacon, the home of his parents.

In bad weather, Lumb wasn't all that cheerful either…the wind could moan for days past the valley's woodlands and obsolete mill chimneys. In winter, the road out might be cut off by snow. There was a story that the long-drop waterfall, which Lumb Bank overlooked, was haunted by the ghosts of dead babies. According to Jeff Nuttall, a poet, artist, actor (and all the rest) who knew the valley, it was also a place 'charged with what Lorca called duende...an atmosphere dense with some primal violence. Lots of people won't go there.'[iii]

At this time, Plath was pregnant and homesick, and Hughes' account paints a picture of the locality as she would have seen it, a gloomy lost world of closed-up shops, defunct chapels - somewhere that was the 'fallen-in grave of its history.' It's hard to imagine how dismal and out-of-time the surroundings were in the late 1950s / early 1960s, the scarcity of jobs, entire rows of houses abandoned, scores of old textile mills collapsing to ruin. For some people, the area around Hebden Bridge appeared to be 'one of the dead ends of ugliness.'[iv]

Although Hughes and Plath made a number of visits to his family home, including several Christmases, the location features little in her poetry, perhaps eight poems in all with Yorkshire settings. In "Hardcastle Crags", collected in *The Colossus*, she describes Heptonstall as a 'dream-peopled village' and beyond it (as the poet is walking up over Cross Hill by moonlight) 'The whole landscape / loomed absolute as the antique world was / once…'. The poem also raises warnings; that piercing wind that could pare 'her' to 'a pinch of flame', the menacing weight of the surrounding hills of stone.[v]

Before the poem was formed, Plath had written to her mother that she had 'never been so happy in my life! It is wild and lonely and a perfect place to work and read. I am basically a nature loving recluse.' In fact, the charm quickly wore off, and subsequent visits became less and less cordial. For Plath and Hughes, it turned out to be easier to love nature and raise a family in Devon, where the summers were longer, the landscape gentler and the pulse of London didn't feel so remote.[vi]

None of that, of course, was enough to preserve the marriage or save Plath's life. Seven months after a suicidal gesture in July 1962 (when she drove her car into a river) she would die in London from deliberate gas inhalation. Hughes chose to have her body buried in Heptonstall churchyard and thereafter began to live, irregularly, with Assia Wevill, an exotic-looking, already married, advertising copywriter. Wevill nurtured more serious ideas about herself than writing advertisements for 'bad bakery bread', which was how Plath rated her rival's abilities.

In fact, she would capably translate a collection of Yehuda Amachai's poems for publication, collaborate with Hughes on a film script and begin to write her own poetry. There are only a few examples of verse in a published selection of Wevill's writing but ample evidence of intellect and a gift for language. During her wilful and adventurous life, she had become fluent in five of them.[vii]

Hughes was still coveting Lumb Bank and repeated the offer of living there together to Wevill, an idea that she thought even less of than Plath. She was cosmopolitan through and through and, as if they needed another reason, her city airs didn't endear her to Hughes' parents.

Perhaps most troubling of all, Lumb Bank was only a short walk from Plath's austere grave. In this sort of primal land, as Emily Bronte suggested, bad weather was not the only thing that might come beating at the night windows.

Although Wevill hoped to accomplish more with her own writing, possibly benefitting from Hughes' editorial oversight and connections, suicide had obliged his attention to Plath's legacy before all else. She also knew, whether in literary works or wifehood, she would always be measured against Plath, whose death, in the opinion of some, was her fault.

With several marriages in her wake, Wevill could hardly have reckoned on the Euripidean drama that would follow her poaching the affections of / being seduced by Hughes; nor that she would have to cope with him grief-stricken and ever-faithless. Killing herself and their daughter Shura on 23 March 1969, was a crueller replication of Plath's own death. Hughes expressed more than anguish when he later wrote, 'When her grave opened its ugly mouth / Why didn't you just fly / Wrap yourself in your hair and make yourself scarce, / Why did you kneel down at the grave's edge / To be identified / Accused and convicted…'[viii]

In that same year, after his mother also died, Hughes finally purchased Lumb Bank. He had imagined it becoming the hub of a creative community, perhaps tempting Gerald, his much-missed brother, to come back from Australia and manage it as a farm. The plan didn't work out and even to him the place began to feel 'oppressive'. Although he never made public what happened to the ashes of Assia and Shura, clues have been found in *Capriccio*, his short, very limited edition collection of poems, that they were scattered in the Colden Valley.[ix]

Hughes continued to spend more of his out-of-London time in Devon, where Carole Orchard, his future wife, lived. He became interested in the Devon-based Arvon Foundation, a charity that organised writing workshops and retreats and, by 1971, had begun to develop plans for Lumb Bank to become its northern course centre. [x] Arvon, he considered 'the first thing of its kind in Britain since the colleges of the old Celtic world.' [xi]

Elements of Lumb - the name, its moody atmosphere and nearby village-life undercurrents - were adopted into Hughes' book-length poem *Gaudete*. The Reverend Nicholas Lumb, an Anglican minister, is abducted by 'elemental spirits' and substituted in the vicarage by a sexually-overwound changeling. The original Lumb is put through a Mithraic rite of tauroctony, a bull sacrifice, intended to bring fertility, rebirth, even a 'new cosmic order', but his smothering in bull entrails and gore is almost a piece of Viennese Actionist performance art. When Lumb finally returns to the world in the epilogue, he has transformed into a poet.

Gaudete's characters are stock country folk, from squires to peasants, a ribald commedia turning to Jacobean tragedy. As the Hughes' scholar Ann Skea put it, the poem immerses us, just like Lumb, in 'the sounds, the smells, the disorientation of pain, the heat of animal bodies, the feel and the cling of blood, mud and water and the sheer abundance of plant and animal life...'[xii]

One of his darkest and most cryptic works, *Gaudete* is a fantasia of infidelity, sacramental orgy, sacrifices and suicide. Since Hughes believed that poetry could be a shamanistic 'working', an invocation, this is one of the works, like *Birthday Letters* and the never-finished *Crow* ('He loved her and she loved him / His kisses sucked out her whole past and future or tried to / He had no other appetite / She bit him she gnawed him she sucked / She wanted him complete inside her / Safe and sure forever and ever…'[xiii]) where the curious find what they think are secrets, where vigilantes find confessions of guilt, where the willing find remorse, and where the poet sought catharsis.

<>

'Foolish enough to have been a poet' is a headstone inscription that sometimes catches the eyes of visitors to Heptonstall's newest graveyard. The name of the man buried there, 'Asa Benveniste', also has an unusual ring. The surname indicates a Sephardic Jewish ethnicity and is more commonly seen in Spain or France . It means "You have arrived well" and the Benveniste who ended up here first arrived in the world 3300 miles away - in 1925 - in the Bronx borough of New York City.

After serving with the US Army in Europe during WWII, Benveniste decided to stay on in Paris, among hundreds of American expatriates, many of whom wanted to become writers or, for a while, to live like they were. A few, that had the money, started little magazines. Along with George Solomos, he put together the first two issues of *Zero*, a quarterly that attracted contributions from Samuel Beckett, James Baldwin and Paul Bowles.

He then moved on, to England, and began to develop his own poetic practices, working with the *I Ching*, the Tarot and other arcane sources. After finding a base in London, he settled into a lifestyle of decadent austerity - living on whiskey, wine, strong American cigarettes, black coffee, and the occasional pizza.[xiv]

With his Cornish wife Pip, an artist and designer, Asa founded the Trigram Press in 1965, the same year that the *International Poetry Incarnation* was held at the Albert Hall. The initial purpose of the *Incarnation* was to showcase Allen Ginsberg in the largest performance space in London. Gregory Corso and Lawrence Ferlinghetti happened to be around so the event developed into an intersection of American and British Beat, Black Mountain College and post-Beat Underground poetry (with a few hip Europeans and a Cuban included for good measure). An audience of about 7000 turned up for an exuberant stoned word-rave, which may have gone off organisationally half-cocked but succeeded in rousing the spirits of England's tentative alternative society.

Iain Sinclair's later appraisal of the event noted that the audience had come for simplistic poetic 'formulations' like those from Adrian

Mitchell rather than the visionary ravings of Harry Fainlight. 'What they wanted, as ever, was a protest prom, Poetry as CND sloganeering.'[xv]

Much of the material for Trigram's publications would arrive through the transatlantic poets' network, producing collections by Piero Heliczer, Tom Raworth, Anselm Hollo, David Meltzer, and Jonathan Williams. Asa would have hated for Trigram's books to be judged simply on appearances, but between him, Pip and his stepson Paul, the publications were made aesthetically beautiful - 'audacious, elegant and legible' – in the words of Jeff Nuttall, one of Asa's friends and another poet that he published. You could say the content had a lot to live up to and vice versa, and it partly did so through Asa's choice of artists and writers who worked in what he called 'acute conditions of exile, living and thinking on the edge of society.'

Jack Hirschman, an old friend from Benveniste's Bronx childhood, caught up with him in London, where they discovered a mutual interest in a poetry involving esoteric investigation and divination. Hirschman described Asa's technique as 'Bop Kabbala', borrowing a term from Ginsberg.[xvi]

Benveniste later said that the ten years he spent engaged in studies of 'Kabbalistic congruities' was a dark period in his life and as a corrective, he moved on to poetry that relished the 'silliness' of domestic life – and in this he had uncovered a 'complex comedy of language.'[xvii]

In Benveniste's presence, you could sense his edgy intensity about words and their disposition. Michael Schmidt, publisher of the international poetry imprint Carcanet, described him as frightening to be around. But there was an undeniably sensitive side, one that came out in the company of old friends. Once, after a long afternoon of wine and jazz, when recollecting the writer B.S. Johnson, he began to weep. Johnson had committed suicide in 1973, aged 40, partly because of what he regarded as an insufficient appreciation of his literary genius. Trigram had published a collection of his poetry and, for the only time, a novel, *House Mother Normal*.

After his death, Johnson developed something of a cult following - readers who have proved to be almost as devoted as Sylvia Plath's but with only a fraction of the numbers. His poetry is less well regarded than his often confessional novels and self-interrogating short films. Even so, he was the *Transatlantic Review* 's poetry editor and a critic for *Ambit*. On the publication of *Ariel,* Plath's first posthumous collection, he was entranced, sensing levels that would take years to fully understand. In fact, he appears to have been confounded by many of the poems, out of his depth, and declared that any review that he or anyone else wrote would be 'irrelevant, unimportant and useless: the book simply *is.*' There were some poems he found 'overwhelmingly moving' but regarded them, too simply, as the outcome of Plath's 'disastrous personal crisis'.[xviii] The tragic immortality that Plath achieved, post-*Ariel*, may have crossed his mind that day as he sat in his bath with a razor and a bottle of brandy.

Trigram became one of the key publishers of the British Poetry Revival, an establishment-shaking movement that attracted most attention from around 1960 to 1977. Largely 'conducted' by the critic, poet and professor Eric Mottram, the Revival could be crudely said to have encouraged poets to take risks and defy conventions. Slightly less crudely, it was a making of poems that listened to themselves rather than duplicating the received forms and tones of how poetry was supposed to be. We'll never know what Plath might have thought of it, but Hughes was sometimes happy to mingle in the Revival's rough little magazines.

Al Alvarez, who was the influential poetry editor of The *Observer* for 10 years, was unimpressed. He had launched his own revision of the British poetry agenda in 1962 with the Penguin anthology *The New Poetry*, where Hughes featured as a leading light. Because of their influence on his chosen native poets, Alvarez bent the rules to allow in two Americans, Robert Lowell and John Berryman. They played to his idea that the impersonality and 'gentility' that prevailed in English poetry was holding it back; that there could be a direct connection between the poet's life experience ('sometimes on the edge of disintegration and breakdown') and the poet's work. In the 1964 second edition, he shrewdly included Plath and Anne Sexton.

The New Poetry was a studied approach to upgrading The Movement, an exclusively English faction of poets from the 1950s that opposed the 'excesses' of American-style Modernism, including its ambiguity, showy word-play, and metaphysics - particularly as they saw it practiced by the 'pretentious' Dylan Thomas.

Interviewed in 1962, Plath had cited Thomas as one of the poets she most admired, along with William Butler Yeats and, increasingly, William Blake. Contemporary English poetry she found to be in a 'straitjacket' and supported Alvarez's complaint about the inhibitions of 'gentility'. The poet peers who excited her most were American, such as Sexton and Lowell, especially his 'intense breakthrough into very serious, very personal, emotional experience, which I feel has been partly taboo.'[xix] In a short piece titled "Context", she had already declared, 'The poets I delight in are possessed by their poems as by the rhythms of their own breathing.'[xx]

Taboo and excess were what the British Poetry Revival thrived on and was, from its origins, willingly American infected. It revelled in academic disapproval, was adept at self-publishing and circulation, welcomed a spectrum of regional and socially diverse voices, and was unrestrained in subject or form. It was also (somewhat) more open to female poets than the preceding literary movements, groups or coteries.

For Alvarez it was a continuation of the Beat Generation, whom he scorned for the drugs and cult of personality (Ginsberg) - '...instead of using their art to redeem the mess they had made of their lives...served the mess up uncooked and called it poetry.'[xxi]

'Howls of protest heard from the shires at this unwanted double influx of domestic experimentalists and Americans,' was how Ken Edwards, one of the Revival's leading voices, explained the outcome of what came to be called The Poetry Wars. The Arts Council of Great Britain cleared the rabble out of the Poetry Society and took back control (from Mottram) of *The Poetry Review*, the Society's magazine. Mainstream presses and the academies were reconfirmed as gatekeepers between the big top and the avant-garde sideshow, with its mountebanks and freaks. A number of Arts Council grants were withdrawn, including Trigram's, and Benveniste began to spend more days at his typewriter.[xxii]

The first time he came to Heptonstall was in the early 1980s having been invited by the Arvon Foundation to lead a residential course at Lumb Bank. The surrounding area was no longer the ghost vale once pictured by Hughes. Its regeneration followed an influx of artists, writers, academics and creative staffers from regional television companies, attracted by low-cost but characterful housing. Migrants also included a Hippy diaspora more interested in the vacant, easily squatted, no-cost housing. The resulting countercultural, artistic mix was the foundation of a café life, antiques & retro, craft-making, organic / artisan food, Lesbian / Gay business community that slowly boho-charmed the rundown town of Hebden Bridge into a visitor destination.

With his new partner, Agneta Falk, Benveniste found a house in Hebden, set up the ground floor as a bookshop and mostly stocked it from his own library. The Poltroon Press publisher Alistair Johnston came to Heptonstall in 1982 - pursuing a project to collect selfies at famous poets' graves. For fun he also photographed Asa, crouching behind Plath's headstone like a Kilroy-was-here imp.[xxiii] This clowning was purely for the camera, not a mockery of her work or its advancement into the canon, and not even a jest in the direction of Plath's attendant faithful. Eight years later, he was to be buried in a plot only a few paces away.

The elegies that followed his death, on 13 April 1990, included one by Roy Fisher,[xxiv] a poem that concludes with a jazzy eye-witness report of the cortege of outsider poets, artists and actors who attended Heptonstall Church for a performance celebration of his life - and then the bacchanalian wake, with 'barrelhouse music' and where the clocks were not the only things that became 'unhitched'.

In contrast, Plath's funeral had been short and sombre. A small service in a Hebden Bridge undertaker's chapel was followed by another in

Heptonstall Church. In attendance were Hughes, his father, a few family members, and two friends from London. From Plath's side came only her brother Warren and his wife.

The most basic death notices had appeared in the London press, with the pointed exception of "A Poet's Epitaph" by Alvarez in the *Observer*. Alongside three of Plath's most recently completed poems, he described the state of mind that had produced them, suggesting that this had moved her towards a certain fate. Whilst writing 'almost as if possessed', she had concentrated on, what he believed, was a 'narrow violent area, between the viable and the impossible, between experience which can be transmuted into poetry and that which is overwhelming.'

Four months earlier, in an interview for the BBC, Plath had also claimed 'experience' as the subject of her latest poems, but as something she felt confident and happy about. Even if drawn from highly 'sensuous and emotional experiences' she expected to control the 'most terrific' ones, even 'madness' or 'being tortured', and still be able to 'manipulate these experiences with an informed and an intelligent mind'.[xxv]

<>

As far-flung as Heptonstall then seemed from the contemporary world, once *Ariel* had been published, it didn't take long for her burial site to attract visitors. At this time, contemporary poetry books were something of a publishing conceit, a way for mainstream publishers to add an unprofitable touch of literary seriousness to their lists. Even 'successful' new poetry collections might sell only 50 or 100 copies per year. Faber and Faber was one of the few London imprints that specialised in poetry and their 3,100 first print run of *Ariel* sold out quickly and, within 10 months, sales reached 15,000 copies.

After almost 60 years, thousands of people (from every part of the world) have been to Plath's grave, many of them making repeat trips.

With a modest published output (four slim poetry collections, one novel, collected stories, and journals – later added to with 'Selected' and 'Collected' editions, diary pages and letters she might rather have kept to herself)[xxvi] she became what waggish publishers' accountants call 'an industry' as her fame achieved critical mass.

The bulk of material has come from others – multiple biographies, documentaries, a biopic, essays, enough theses to choke a library, conferences, seminars, festivals, encyclopaedia entries and other devotions. And, to her mother's displeasure, her grave not only came to be treated as a shrine, but one that more obsessive devotees thought they were entitled to an opinion about.[xxvii]

Regarding the confiscation of Plath's life and work, her daughter Frieda made herself clear in the poem "Readers". 'While their mothers lay in quiet graves / Squared out by those green cut pebbles / And flowers in a jam jar, they dug mine up.' And then, 'They scooped out her eyes to see how she saw, / And bit away her tongue in tiny mouthfuls / To speak with her voice.'[xxviii] With more detachment, the poetry critic Christina Patterson called, 'The sanctification and widespread appropriation of Sylvia Plath…one of the more peculiar cultural phenomena of the 20th century.'[xxix] More recently Dr Ruth Cain wrote that Plath had 'opened her inner life via her writing, but as Hughes (and later her daughter) argued, she would not necessarily have wanted strangers advocating for a false version of her, an avatar created to validate their various tribal arguments.'[xxx]

Between the excitable fanbase and academics picking over the words for epigrams and criminal evidence, the poems' purposes for Plath and even the purpose of poetry itself can get lost in the rhetorical smoke. Plath made a point of saying that she wasn't inspired by social issues, was not writing 'headline poetry' but was moved by things such as a child forming, 'finger by finger', 'the hurt and wonder of loving', and the 'bleakness of the moon over a yew tree in a neighbouring graveyard.' For her, the greatest use of poetry was in 'its pleasure--not its influence as a religious or political propaganda.'[xxxi]

There are those who, in the Calvinist, desiccating vocabulary of Theory-speak, lithe and nuanced as a coroner's report, have tried to conscript Plath's writing as testament for a certain, cold-blooded form of Feminism. Mostly, this demonstrates how much a language of formulae can debase a language of spells - the creation of which relies on passion, instinct, and chance.

'The artist is extremely lucky who is presented with the worst possible ordeal which will not actually kill him, At that point, he's in business,' are the words of the Pulitzer Prize-winning poet John Berryman. Finally, his own ordeals with depression and alcohol did not spare him, nor his poetry keep him alive – he leapt to his death on 7 January 1973.

The label of Confessional Poet was one Berryman rejected. For young poets subsequently drawn to the category's glamour, the question was whether their own troubled childhoods, breakdowns, or ruinous conduct could inspire poesy that was up to snuff. There have always been bohemian suicide clubs, the seductive beauty of the pale and doomed, the Almost Dead Poets

Society, the example of Hart Crane flinging himself overboard. Andrei Codrescu, an editor and poet who also taught university poetry classes, explained the problem, '…if I let them write about whatever they want instead of insisting on the mortal gravity of the art they'd signed up for, everything they'd write would be about suicide and mass murder…They are young, these people, but not above extorting emotions from fake traumas.'[xxxii]

For Robert Lowell, Plath, Sexton, Berryman, the clinically intervened neuroses were real and the life injuries more than Confessionally adequate. As Sexton remarked of the conversations she and Plath had during martini nourished afternoons, following their attendance at Lowell's writing workshops, 'We talked death with burned-up intensity, both of us drawn to it like moths to an electric light bulb. Sucking on it.'xxxiii

If Plath had lived longer, she also might have disowned Confessionalism and associations with austere versions of Feminism. Like Sexton, she regarded herself as a self-defining poet and a (sometimes) resilient woman that so happened to live with / suffer from the conventions of the post-war, American middleclass for females - its expectations of subservience, a prevailing sense of duty, and respectability. Sexton argued against a skewed labelling of her work, how only the 'hate men' poems were selected for 'women's lib' anthologies. 'Naturally there are times when I hate men, who wouldn't? But there are times when I love them.'[xxxiv]

When Plath and Hughes were first married, new acquaintances were often over-conscious of his imposing personality and, since she was she was so good at being the genial and supportive wife, they would forget or ignore that she was also a poet.

Ben Sonnenberg was another of those Europe-roaming Americans who wanted to be a writer. Although less successful as a playwright than as a trust-funded playboy, he eventually founded and edited a literary magazine, the New York-based *Grand Street*.[xxxv] When introduced to Hughes, he was only 22 and became as enthralled by Hughes' aura, energy and baritone voice as by his

lodestone talent. Following a meal at the Hughes'
London flat, Sonnenberg claimed to remember
little about Plath except that she '...expected too
much applause for the dinner she'd cooked and
too much approval for the economy of her and
Ted's arrangement.'xxxvi

A year after her first suicide attempt and the
resulting six months of psychiatric treatment,
Plath had written a letter of reassurance to her
mother. 'I am really regrettably
unoriginal, conventional and puritanical…(a)
clock-regulated, responsible, salad-eating, water-
drinking, bed-going, economical, practical girl.'
Of course, she turned out to be so much more, but
when Plath and Sexton set out to make their
marks in the literary establishment, they would

have been expected to attend to domestic responsibilities and curtail their natural vitalities.

In *The Bell Jar* Plath examined the difficult choices faced by warm-blooded young women of promise - from coping with socially enforced identities to the risks of sexual experience in the days before the contraceptive pill. Her characters struggling to control their libidos might go mad. Ones that gave in to it were likely to come to a bad end, often the kind that involved an unsuitable relationship - or two. Creatively gifted and intelligent girls have been known to follow their wilder impulses, unable to resist rogues and bad boys. Emily Prager, a writer, actress and consummate New York City culturati star, proposed, '...there is nothing that warms a smart girl's heart like the smile on the face of a sadist.'[xxxvii]

Plath was something of a serial romantic (although hardly a patch on Sexton) and one winter's night at Cambridge, she expressed unsisterly ideas in a journal entry, '...a woman, I fight all women for my men. My men. I am a woman, and there is no loyalty, even between mother and daughter.' [xxxviii] Defiance or evidence of a deeper insecurity? Something anyway to make us feel even more compassion for her last difficult months of life, the heartsickness, the fatigue of looking after the children, the compulsive intensity of writing - coping with the unnaturally cold weather, her illnesses and depression and mis-managed medication.

Plath had lost lovers before but losing Hughes, both soulmate and her star-twinned genius, was devastating…especially losing him to a competitor of such abnormal allure. In her poem "The Rival", she dissected Assia in cool detail when comparing her to the moon. 'You leave the same impression / Of something beautiful, but annihilating.'[xxxix] Hughes maintained that they had both been entranced with Weevil's caressing eyes and 'many blooded beauty', the way she was 'slightly filthy with erotic mystery'[xl] and irresistibly dangerous.

As a frequenter of literary graves, Patti Smith has visited the last resting places of Anne Bronte, Bertolt Brecht, Jean Genet, Leon Trotsky, William Burroughs, Jim Morrison, and Elvis. Across Arthur Rimbaud's tomb she bopped like a boneyard angel at the afterlife disco, maybe singing that broken rhyme of her own creation, 'rimbaud rimbaud facing the wall / cold as hail dead as a doornail'.[xli] She has been to sit quietly alongside Plath on at least three occasions, one of them in the dead of Winter, bringing in tribute a notebook, a purple ribbon and a sock embroidered with a bee. But Plath, who Smith once described as having 'hair worthy of a Breck commercial and the incisive observational powers of a female surgeon cutting out her own heart', wasn't the poet who set the example for Smith's tangled subterranean days in New York - her punkish antics and performances at CBGB.

Diane di Prima's *Memoirs of a Beatnik* is a title I came across in Asa Benveniste's bookshop and, braving his displeasure for anyone who actually bought any of his stock, took it home. *Memoirs* is more salaciously straight-to-the-point than the Olympia Press 'dirty books' written by, let's say, William Burroughs or Gregory Corso. Di Prima mixes her raunch with satire and more than a little autobiography - possibly including the extempore orgy involving Ginsberg and Jack Kerouac. When taking a breather, she puts the 50s' hip scene into perspective, which, by today's standards, sounds fairly tame. 'As far as we knew, there was only a small handful of us – perhaps forty or fifty in the city – who knew what we knew, who raced about in Levis and work shirts, smoked dope, dug the new jazz, spoke a bastardization of the black argot.'

While Plath was studying hard and being ambitious at Smith, set on an Academic career as much as a poetic one, di Prima was at Swarthmore; both of them notably swell joints among blue-chip liberal arts colleges. After a year, di Prima dropped out and plunged into New York's Lower East Side, to the '…centre of a queer kinship network, of 'men with lipstick,/women with crew cuts... Junkies and jazz musicians – artists as outlaws, and outlaws as artists.'[xlii]

When someone handed her a small black and white booklet, the newly published *Howl and other Poems*, di Prima read the signs of an enormous change coming. 'It followed that if there was one Allen, there must be more, other people writing what they heard, living, however obscurely and shamefully, what they knew.'[xliii] She had no illusions about the boy gang she was running with, where chicks were muses, beds of convenience, and subsidizers…where those, like her, who were also poets, had a harder time getting their space on the page or the coffee-house stage. Di Prima defined her relationships to suit her own interests and kept her independence, even in child rearing.

Once di Prima had considered the subject of departed poets and their graves in a swinging, anti-eulogistic poem, which includes, 'Eating yr words / eating yr hat / eating the wet hat of a dead poet / in a cemetery full of dismembered freezers...'[xliv]

In 1953, while still at Smith, Plath published a poem, "Mad Girl's Love Song", with the Punk attitude opening line, 'I shut my eyes and the world drops dead'. It goes on in brazen empathy for the stray life of bohemian romance, 'I dreamed that you bewitched me into bed / And sung me moon-struck, kissed me quite insane / (I think I made you up inside my head.)' It's a wonder it's never been set to music.[xlv]

<>

At Plath's grave visitors have yet to be seen eating hats, but curious behaviour is not unknown. They often come bearing tokens - some of reverence, some of vanity; poems they've written, love notes, copies of theses, a tributary stream of small change in glamorous currencies, bouquets, and deep-red Revlon lipsticks. Left alone, this would quickly become a mess, a collection of litter, scrap and symbolic offerings, spilling over onto nearby plots.

The most frequent 'gifts' are pencils or pens, crowded into small pots or firmly planted in the charmed earth. Probably they are something like votives: the candles, pilgrim marks and effigies that were once placed on shrines or the tombs of saints.

It's not for nothing that the earliest church at Heptonstall was dedicated to Thomas a' Becket. After martyrdom, it only took two years for Becket to be canonized, making his cult a sure-thing franchise and ensuring a steady flow of travellers and offerings in exchange for indulgences. The Roman poet Virgil is a better example – with his empty tomb in Naples frequented by writers (and pagans) for 2000 years. Inside the chamber where his body never rested, visitors scrawl graffiti or ritually burn little notes, giving thanks for Virgil's immortal words and pleading with him to make them better poets.

Blaise Cendrars, a French poet, memoirist and raconteur, even dug a shallow grave in the paddock beside the tomb and slept in it each night for most of a week. Whatever transformation he hoped for with Virgil's assistance, failed to occur.

For the sufficiently obsessed, those 'desperately seeking', a grave can become confused with a portal, a looking-glass mirage, through which the living can contact the absent idol. Plath's poem, "November Graveyard", was inspired by both the place she would finally come to rest and the Gothically shaded graveyard of Haworth. In it, the yearning illusions of an afterlife are inventively conjured but only to be dismissed. 'At the essential landscape stare, stare / Till your eyes foist a vision dazzling on the wind: / Whatever lost ghosts flare, / Damned, howling in their shrouds across the moor'.

<>

In the oldest part of Heptonstall's graveyards, headstones tend to stick to the basics - name and age, family relationships. During the 19th century, for the affluent, intricate remembrances came into fashion, the stonework more detailed and sculpted, with spiritual axioms and symbols of belief and the life eternal. Status and faith-signalling called for larger monuments and provided more money for quarrymen and stonemasons.

When the original Heptonstall church fell into disrepair and struggled to accommodate an increasing number of worshippers, a larger church, St Thomas the Apostle, was built nearby and consecrated in 1854. One effect was to limit the churchyard space available for burials and the congestion of graves is obvious to the south side of the new building. An additional cemetery was donated by the member of a local mill-owning family, using land taken from the village's old field network. Like Boot Hill, it lay exposed to the driving weather and beyond the comfort of the lights.

In the new graveyard, 20th century headstones turned simpler again, and more secular. Plath's is modest enough with her name and dates and the quotation, 'Even Amidst Fierce Flames The Golden Lotus Can Be Planted'. This was possibly from a 16th Century Chinese Buddhist text but Hughes, who chose it, suggested the *Bhagavad Gita*.

At a time and in a place where she would have conventionally been buried only under her married name, Hughes made certain that 'Sylvia Plath Hughes' was used. Over the years, the gravestone has been vandalised by people attempting to remove 'Hughes', unable to appreciate the difference between a private burial place and a public monument.

<>

As a child, Plath had defected from Unitarianism after her father died and only towards the end of her life appears to have reconsidered Christianity. With Hughes, she had collaborated in studies of astrology and the occult, including sessions with a homemade Ouija board that fed into her writing. In her journal of 4 July 1958, she wrote about a board session where she described them having 'more fun than a movie.'[xlvi]

One of Hughes' influences, William Butler Yeats, also in collaboration with his wife, had used spirit writing, a Ouija-like method, to develop his poems. Around the same time as Yeats, the Surrealists adopted automatic writing, inspired by the emerging theories of psychoanalysis, and drawing on the images and language of dreams.

The board, and what Plath referred to as 'Pan', her guide, '...allowed her to shut down her exterior voices so that she might better listen to the interior ones'[xlvii] and from this came material like, 'It is a chilly god, a god of shades, / Rises to the glass from his black fathoms'[xlviii] which then carried on in imagery of Shakespearean rococo. At other times this developed fluency with the lyrically mysterious set forces of pagan nature into her work.

Another esoteric 'tool' that Plath would use in writing was a deck of Tarot cards, given to her by Hughes on her 24th birthday. Almost sixty years after her death, these cards were among some of

Plath's personal effects sold at auction, attracting the interest of specialist dealers in literary artefacts, universities, and lovers of her writing with deep pockets. If there is an 'aura' bestowed by Plath's fingertips and searching concentration, the value of such a thing supposes the haunting imperishable, the supernatural essence that endows precious relics. The Tarot deck had been expected to realise around £6,000 and finally sold for £151,200.[xlix]

Al Alvarez had his own ideas about Plath's dabbling in the supernatural and suggested that this contributed to a mental state that gravitated towards self-destruction. In an extract from his autobiography, with the sensationalist tabloid title, "How Black Magic Killed Sylvia Plath", he portrayed himself as Plath's friend as well as the champion of her work, particularly 'the new style of poetry' she had been writing.

The last time he had seen her alive was on Christmas Eve, just over a month before her suicide. He had been invited around for a meal but said he could only stay for a quick drink, describing her as distressed and dishevelled, with 'a curious , desolate, rapt air, like a priestess emptied out by the rites of a cult.' She had broken into tears and pleaded with him not to leave and the subtext here, which Alvarez discussed in later interviews, is the guilt he felt for refusing a possible intimacy. He claimed that he was unable to help her personally, not able to 'shoulder her despair'.

He then makes an accusation, perhaps to take some of the heat off himself. 'The weird mishmash of pagan superstition and Celtic myth that got him (Hughes) where he wanted to be worked for him…for Sylvia it was a foreign country in every sense…Belief in dark gods and shamans and the baleful influence of the stars didn't come naturally to her…'. Meaningfully, he concludes, '…anything her husband could do, she could do better.'[1]

◇

Today the cemetery looks less forlorn than in 1963, when Plath was buried. The headstones have gathered around her and progressed half a dozen more rows towards the sunrise. The high stone walls on three sides are now shadowed by mature trees and the graves overlooked by the back windows of new housing. In a central space, a small square was created, with compact memorial stones and benches for mourners to reflect, and where Plath's visitors sometimes sit and talk. They are more likely to linger on a day when the weather hawk isn't at its usual local work, scouring stone and bone.

Hughes knew this wuthering energy and its province better than anyone. 'Where the howlings of heaven / Pour down onto earth / Looking for bodies…'[li]

There is no point in looking for him here, among the graves of his mother and father and other kin. His ashes were tipped into another wildness several hundred miles south, near Taw Head on Dartmoor, beyond the reach of the vengeful. Three years later a memorial stone was installed, a large, undressed boulder that looks to have rested there for a thousand years. The lettering of 'Ted Hughes OM / 1930-1998', is so finely inscribed it might be a trick of the light.

For information about
The Arvon Foundation
www.arvon.org

ENDNOTES

[i] Hardcastle Crags is a wooded valley in West Yorkshire that is owned by the National Trust. At its centre is Gibson Mill, built around 1800 and one the first working mills in the Industrial Revolution.

[ii] Heptonstall is a small hilltop village, historically part of the West Riding of Yorkshire. At between 8-900 feet it overlooks nearby Hebden Bridge and is one of the most historic villages in the Pennines.

[iii] "Jeff Nuttall reviews Gaudete", *New Yorkshire Writing*, #3, Winter 1978, Bradford, West Yorkshire. p. 4.

Nuttall was a pioneer of Performance Art in England and he and his collaborator, Rose McGuire, once used Heptonstall as a location for one of their 'Telephone Novel' pieces. This involved a bizarrely dressed McGuire leaving mysterious packages on doorsteps around the village. It was talked about for years and supposed by some to have been acts of attempted witchcraft.

[iv] Ted Hughes, "Introduction", *Singing Brink – An Anthology of Poetry from Lumb Bank*, The Arvon Press, Hebden Bridge, 1987. p.8.

[v] In her 1957 poem, "THE SNOWMAN ON THE MOOR", Plath dramatizes a domestic argument, where 'she' stalks out of the house in a snowy Yorkshire mid-winter, 'intractable as a driven ghost'.

[vi] Elaine Feinstein, *Ted Hughes–The Life of a Poet*, W. W. Norton & Company, New York, 2001. p.70.

[vii] *The Collected Writings of Assia Wevill* appeared in 2021 - lsupress.org/books/detail/collected-writings-of-assia-wevill/. See also

dacapopress.com/titles/yehuda-koren/lover-of-unreason/9780786721054/

[viii] Ted Hughes, "The Error", in *Capriccio*, The Gehenna Press, Northampton, Maine, 1990.

[ix] http://thetedhughessociety.org/capriccio

[x] Elaine Feinstein, *Ted Hughes – The Life of a Poet*, W. W. Norton & Company, New York, 2001. pp. 203-4.

[xi] Ted Hughes, "Introduction", *Singing Brink – An Anthology of Poetry from Lumb Bank*, The Arvon Press, Hebden Bridge, 1987. p.9.

[xii] Ann Skea, "Gaudete and The Reverend Lumb's Parish and Parishioners" *Ted Hughes Society Journal, Vol 4*, 2014.

[xiii] Ted Hughes, "Lovesong" in *Crow*, Faber, London 1999. p. 83.

[xiv] Jeremy Reed, *I Heard It Through The Grapevine, Asa Benveniste and Trigram Press*, Shearsman Books, Bristol 2016. p.13.

[xv] Iain Sinclair, *Lights Out For The Territory*, Granta Publications, London, 1997. p.132.

[xvi] Jack Hirschman, "Kabbala, Communism and Street Level Poiesis" in *Mysticism and Meaning*, ed. Alex S Kohar, Three Pines Press, St Petersburg, Florida, 2019. p.61.

[xvii] Asa Benveniste, "As a Valediction", *Throw Out the Lifeline, Lay Out the Course*, Anvil Press, London, 1983. p.7

[xviii] B.S. Johnson, "Sylvia Plath's *Ariel*", a review in *Ambit*, 24, 1965.

[xix] Interviewed by Peter Orr for the BBC series *The Poet Speaks* on 30 October 1962.

[xx] Sylvia Plath, "Context" in *Johnny Panic and the Bible of Dreams*, Faber and Faber, London, 1979. p.92.

[xxi] Al Alvarez, *The Writer's Voice*, Bloomsbury, London, 2005. p.105.

[xxii] Ken Edwards, *UK Small Press Publishing since 1960: The Transatlantic Axis,* writing.upenn.edu/epc/authors/edwards/edwards_press.html

[xxiii] poltroonpress.com/dead-poets/

[xxiv] Roy Fisher, "At the grave of Asa Benveniste", in *The Long and the Short of It – Poems 1955-2010*, Bloodaxe Books, Tarset, Northumberland, 2012. pp.193-4.

[xxv] Interviewed by Peter Orr for the BBC series *The Poet Speaks* on 30 October 1962.

[xxvi] Also published were some small children's books, including *The Bed Book,* and a number of limited editions. *The Collected Poems* won the 1982 Pulitzer Prize.

[xxvii] Author's interview with Frances Bruce, a former director of Calder Civic Trust, 12.02.22. The Trust had been contacted and asked if the path to Sylvia Plath's grave could be signposted. The Trust wrote to Aurelia Plath for her opinion. In reply she objected to anything of the kind. Although she understood people wanting to see where her daughter was buried and that her writing and her life were 'public', the grave was 'private' and for the family.

[xxviii] Frieda Hughes, "Readers", *POP! The Poetry Olympics Poetry Anthology*, ed. Michael Horovitz, New Departures, London, 2000. pp.64-5.

[xxix] Christina Patterson, "In search of the poet", *The Independent*, 6 February 2004.

[xxx] Email to author, 11 October, 2022.

[xxxi] Sylvia Plath, "Context", *Johnny Panic and the Bible of Dreams*, Faber and Faber, London, 1979. p.92-3.

[xxxii] Andrei Codrescu, *The Poetry Lesson*, Princeton University Press, Princeton, New Jersey, 2010. p.37.

[xxxiii] Diane Wood Middlebrook, *Anne Sexton – A Biography*, Virago Press, London, 1992, p.107.

[xxxiv] Anne Sexton, *No Evil Star, Selected Essays, Interviews, and Prose*, University of Michigan Press, Ann Arbour, 1985. p.179

xxxv *Grand Street* ran from 1981 to 2004, edited by Sonnenberg for the first eight years. Ted Hughes' contributed to the first issue and a number of others, including an essay about Plath's journals and extracts from these.

xxxvi Ben Sonnenberg, *Lost Property – Memoirs and Confessions of a Bad Boy*, Faber and Faber, London, 1991. p.131.

xxxvii Emily Prager, Introduction to *After Claude* by Iris Owens, The New York Review of Books, New York, 2010. p.x.

xxxviii Sylvia Plath, extract from a Journal, *MARS, No. 1,* ed. Kristina Dusseldorp, London, 1978. p.20.

xxxix Sylvia Plath, "The Rival", *Ariel*, Faber and Faber, London, 1968. p.53.

xl Ted Hughes, "Dreamers", in *Birthday Letters*, Faber and Faber, London, 1998. p.157.

xli Patti Smith, "rimbaud dead" in *Babel*, Virago, London, 1978. p.30.

xlii "Stay Home, Stay Stoned", Andrea Brady, *London Review of Books,* 10 March, 2022.

xliii Diane di Prima, *Memoirs of a Beatnik*, Olympia Press, New York, 1969. p.164.

[xliv] Diane di Prima, "Recent Boring Literary Pastimes", in *The Stiffest of the Corpse*, ed. Andrei Codrescu, City Lights Books, San Francisco, 1989. p.186.

[xlv] allpoetry.com/Mad-Girl's-Love-Song

[xlvi] *The Unabridged Journals of Sylvia Plath*, ed. Karin V. Kukil, Anchor Books, New York, 2000. p. 400.

[xlvii] Kailey Tedesco, 'How Sylvia Plath used a Ouija board to write

poetry', ultraculture.org/blog/2016/01/31/sylvia-plath-ouija-board/

[xlviii] Sylvia Plath, "Ouija", *The Colossus*, Faber, London, 1972. p.52.

[xlix] lithub.com/maybe-broccoli-doesnt-like-you-either-lot-151-on-the-allure-of-joan-didions-objects/

[l] Al Alvarez, "How Black Magic Killed Sylvia Plath", in The *Guardian*, London, 15 September 1999.

[li] Ted Hughes, "Where The Mothers" from *Remains of Elmet*, Faber and Faber, London, 1979. p. 10.

Printed in Great Britain
by Amazon

18117504R00047